ALL ABO

THE
FIRST WORLD WAR
1914-1918

PAM ROBSON

HODDER
Wayland

TIMELINE

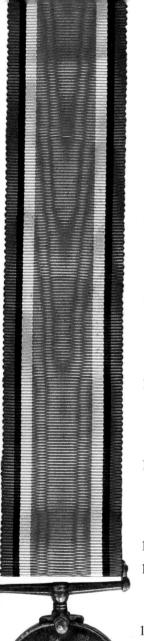

1914
> 28 June *Assassination of Archduke Franz Ferdinand in Sarajevo, Bosnia*
> 4 August *Britain declares war on Germany*
> October *First battle of Ypres, trench warfare begins*
> December *Christmas truce on the battlefield*

1915
> April *The Gallipoli campaign*
> April *Second battle of Ypres*
> May *Sinking of the* Lusitania

1916
> February *The Germans attack the French at Verdun*
> May *Battle of Jutland*
> July *Battle of the Somme*

1917
> March *Russian Revolution*
> April *USA declares war on Germany*
> July *Third battle of Ypres, also called Passchendaele*

1918
> March *Russia makes peace with Germany*
> August *Allied offensive*
> 11 November *Germany surrenders*

1919 *Peace treaty of Versailles*

1920 *An Act of Parliament establishes a permanent home for British war archives in the Imperial War Museum*
> 11 November *Unveiling of the Cenotaph in London*

1992 *Civil war breaks out in Bosnia, the UN steps in to keep the peace*

CONTENTS

POPPIES RED AS BLOOD

For four long years, the ancient Belgian town of Ypres in Flanders was a strategic point on a vast European battlefield that stretched almost as far as Switzerland. Those who were lucky enough to survive the suffering and slaughter of this Great War or First World War, which lasted from 1914 until 1918, returned home with sad memories of red poppies waving to and fro among the graves. Dead soldiers were buried where they fell and the cemeteries of Ypres mark these battlegrounds.

IN FLANDERS FIELDS

In Flanders fields the poppies blow
Between the crosses, row on row,
That mark our place; and in the sky
The larks still bravely singing fly
Scarce heard amid the guns below.

We are the dead. Short days ago
We lived, felt dawn, saw sunset glow,
Loved and were loved, and now we lie
In Flanders fields.

Take up our quarrel with the foe;
To you from failing hands we throw
The torch; be yours to hold it high.
If ye break faith with us who die
We shall not sleep, though poppies grow
In Flanders fields.

John McCrae, 1915

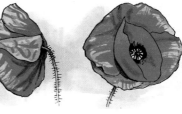

This poem was written in 1915 by a Canadian medical officer on the battlefields of Ypres. He wrote the poem on a page torn from a dispatch book.

In Britain there is a special remembrance day called Poppy Day. It is always the Sunday closest to 11 November. But nowadays we remember the dead of two world wars because in 1939 war broke out again.

War memorials can be seen today in almost every town and village in Britain and France. They carry the names of local men who died in both world wars.

The Cenotaph was unveiled on 11 November 1920 in Whitehall, London, as a symbol of remembrance for those who died in the Great War. Each year after the end of the War a memorial service and parade were held at the Cenotaph at 11 a.m. on the 11th day of the 11th month – the exact time that the War ceased – and there was a two-minute silence. This ceremony now takes place on Poppy Day. Artificial red poppies are also sold to raise money for war widows and wounded soldiers.

MEMORIES OF THE PAST

Few of the soldiers who fought in the Great War are still alive today. Soon it will not be possible to hear first-hand accounts of the dreadful events of 1914-18. We can still read the letters and diaries of young soldiers, many of whom later died in battle. Sepia photographs exist – some taken by official photographers and others by soldiers who smuggled a camera to the battle front. During the Great War, British families watched the Pathé News at the cinema or scanned newspapers for stories from the front. There was no public radio or television. Now we can look back at those news items in archives. Museums hold other fascinating artefacts given by bereaved families.

The name of the Imperial War Museum honours the dominions and colonies of the old British Empire, whose soldiers fought alongside British troops from the 'mother country'.

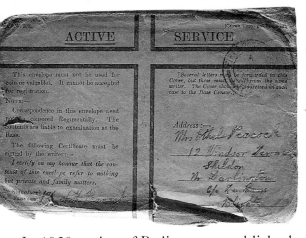

These 'green cross' envelopes contained uncensored letters. Soldiers had to promise that the letters contained only personal information.

Private Arthur Peacock of the Durham Light Infantry regularly wrote to his young wife, Ethel. He was killed in action in 1917 and so never returned to his wife and their two baby sons.

In 1920 an Act of Parliament established a permanent home for British war archives when the Imperial War Museum was set up in London.

Mrs Ethel Peacock
12 Windsor Terrace
Shildon
Nr Darlington
C/o Durham
Blighty

I will write again to morrow Ethel ta ta ta

With Love & kisses to my
Wife. I am leaving to day
so do look after yourself & the
God above knows where we will b
but I will try to keep a good hear
I want you to do the same Ethel S
so Good Bye dear one
Hoped you will give

On Active Service

WITH THE BRITISH
EXPEDITIONARY FORCE

Y.M.C.A.

10th Letter   May 31st 1917

Dearest Wife & Son.

Just a few lines to you hoping you are keeping
in good Health as it leaves me at present very well, I
am in a good heart to night Ethel, I got your letter & the Photo
& it has eased my mind a great I can tell you. I know we are
both alike Ethel, in wanting letters. I will write you as often
as I can, every day in fact without something comes in my road
& stops me, & you write to me as often as you can Ethel. Well
Ethel . . . . I have got the bandage off

9

'RULE BRITANNIA'

T oday the countries of Europe are working for unity through co-operation with each other. In 1914, Europe dominated the world but each European country was striving to be more powerful than its neighbour. Many of these countries held colonies all over the world. Britain, France and Germany were struggling for dominance in Africa. During the Boer War in South Africa (1899-1902) the Germans supported the Boers against the British.

The British navy was the most powerful in the world in 1914, but the idea that 'Britannia rules the waves' is no longer appropriate in today's world. Few British children now know the name 'Britannia' because it belongs to a past era.

Many countries within the British Empire, including India, sent troops to fight with the British during the Great War of 1914-18.

At that time the British Empire extended worldwide from Canada to Australia, with a total population of over 500 million people. When war was declared in 1914, soldiers from the dominions and colonies of the Empire flocked to support the 'mother country'.

THE BRITISH EMPIRE IN 1914
British territories are coloured pink

RICH AND POOR

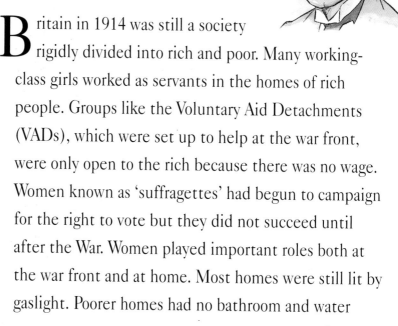

B ritain in 1914 was still a society
rigidly divided into rich and poor. Many working-
class girls worked as servants in the homes of rich
people. Groups like the Voluntary Aid Detachments
(VADs), which were set up to help at the war front,
were only open to the rich because there was no wage.
Women known as 'suffragettes' had begun to campaign
for the right to vote but they did not succeed until
after the War. Women played important roles both at
the war front and at home. Most homes were still lit by
gaslight. Poorer homes had no bathroom and water
came from a
tap in the
wall.

*Policemen
arresting a
suffragette
protester
outside
Buckingham
Palace in
London.*

Outside, in streets choked with smoke from coal fires, there were horse-drawn cabs, bicycles, trams and the new motor buses, but few motor cars.

In 1914, hats were worn by both sexes. Male headwear indicated social class – flat caps (working class), boaters (upper class) and trilbies (middle class). When men queued to enlist as soldiers the mix of headwear indicated a new sense of equality. Rich women wore large hats held in place with long hat pins.

Poor people lived in slums like the one shown here.

FRIENDS AND ENEMIES

K aiser Wilhelm II of Germany was the grandson of Queen Victoria of Britain. Most of the royal families of Europe were related by marriage. The Kaiser wanted Germany to be the strongest country in Europe. When Germany began to expand its navy, the supremacy of the British at sea was threatened. France had already been an enemy of Germany for some time.

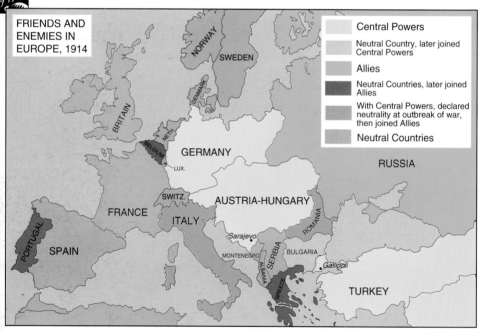

FRIENDS AND ENEMIES IN EUROPE, 1914

- Central Powers
- Neutral Country, later joined Central Powers
- Allies
- Neutral Countries, later joined Allies
- With Central Powers, declared neutrality at outbreak of war, then joined Allies
- Neutral Countries

NORWAY · SWEDEN · BRITAIN · DENMARK · NETH. · BELGIUM · GERMANY · LUX. · RUSSIA · SWITZ. · AUSTRIA-HUNGARY · FRANCE · ITALY · ROMANIA · *Sarajevo* · PORTUGAL · SPAIN · MONTENEGRO · ALBANIA · SERBIA · BULGARIA · *Gallipoli* · GREECE · TURKEY

Germany and Austria-Hungary had formed an alliance. They were joined by Italy to form the Triple Alliance of the Central Powers. Russia, France and Britain formed the Triple Entente to oppose them. When war broke out in 1914, Italy remained neutral and then joined the Triple Entente powers – the 'allies' – in April 1915.

On 28 June 1914 the heir to the Austrian throne, Archduke Franz Ferdinand, and his wife, the Duchess Sophie, were assassinated in Sarajevo, Bosnia, by the Serbian terrorist Gavrilo Princip.

Central Europe was dominated by Germany and by Austria-Hungary – this was an empire of many nationalities, including Serbs. In the east the Czar ruled the vast country of Russia – another empire of different nationalities. Long before 1914 two opposing groups of alliances had taken shape in Europe. The spark that ignited conflict between them was the assassination in Bosnia of the heir to the Austrian throne.

Kaiser Wilhelm II and his British cousin King George V together in 1913.

WAR IS DECLARED

The Treaty of London (1839) guaranteed Belgian neutrality and had been signed by Britain.

E xactly one month after the assassination in Sarajevo, the Austro-Hungarians attacked Serbia. Russian armies mobilised to defend Serbia. Germany promptly launched an attack on Russia's ally, France. On 4 August Britain had to declare war on Germany because German troops had swept down towards France through the neutral country of Belgium. After witnessing the crowds outside his palace, King George V wrote in his diary: "When they heard that war had been declared...the cheering was terrific." Belgium's resistance and Russia's readiness for war led to the failure of the German plan, but British and French troops were pushed back as the Germans moved south. The battle of the Marne was fought so close to Paris that French troops were ferried to the battle front in taxis. Eventually the Germans were pushed back.

The German Schlieffen Plan aimed for a quick defeat of the French, in the belief that the Russians would be slow to prepare for war. Germany then intended to move east to attack Russia.

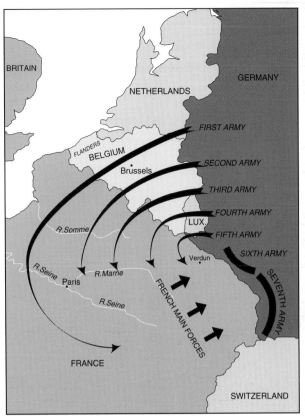

Crowds gathered outside the Houses of Parliament to hear the declaration of war. People in Britain believed that the War would be over by Christmas. Britons travelling in mainland Europe after war had been declared had to obtain documents to travel home. Passports became essential for the first time.

THE CALL TO ARMS

'The Old Contemptibles' were experienced soldiers. They formed the first BEF that held up the German advance at the battle of Mons. Most of them were killed in the early months of the War.

B ritain's regular soldiers were sent to fight a war they expected to be over by Christmas. But by 1917 it had become a world war. These soldiers were nicknamed 'The Old Contemptibles' after the Kaiser called them 'that contemptible little army'. They formed the first British Expeditionary Force (BEF).

British propaganda like this made fun of the Kaiser.

Newly enlisted British soldiers were nicknamed 'Tommies' after Thomas Atkins – a fictional soldier who was listed in an army account book. New recruits often had to wear a blue serge uniform jacket because khaki was in short supply. This was called a 'Kitchener Blue'.

Lord Kitchener led a recruitment drive and thousands of men joined his 'new armies'. After training, often using only dummy weapons, these troops entered the war in 1915. Men who did not enlist as soldiers were sometimes handed a white feather as an insult. After conscription was introduced in 1916, some of these conscientious objectors were shot. Millions of men from Britain and the British Empire served in the Great War. The Australian Prime Minister said: "Remember that when the Empire is at war so is Australia at war."

REMEMBER BELGIUM

ENLIST TO-DAY

Friends who enlisted together were allowed to form special 'Pals' battalions. This was why some small towns and villages in Britain lost all their young men.

19

INTRODUCING DORA

The British government acted immediately on the outbreak of war and introduced the Defence of the Realm Act (DORA), which gave it powers to take over factories, mines and transport for the war effort. Conscription was delayed until 1916 when the Military Service Act was passed. Britain's railways were taken into public control – they were vital for transporting troops and supplies. In 1915 the National Registration Act made it necessary for all British civilians between the ages of 15 and 65 to carry an identity card. Women became a vital part of the workforce in the war effort, taking over the jobs of men who had enlisted.

DORA gave the British government sweeping powers.

Women of the Land Army unloading sacks of grain.

By 1915 all hopes of a quick victory had faded and munitions factories employed thousands of people making guns and explosives. It was not until 1916 that food shortages were felt in Britain.

British national registration card.

On the eve of war, Britain's gold coinage was replaced by paper currency. Two old ten-shilling notes were worth £1.

CAVALRY VERSUS GUNS

A British captain described his first sight of French
soldiers on horseback: "...they were in their full
cuirassier dress: enormous white metal helmet with
horsehair hangings; breastplate covered with cloth,
over a dark blue tunic; red breeches and black leggings.
They advanced to the line in single file carrying a
carbine like a popgun, in the left hand, and a lance in
the right, and an enormous sabre was hooked up on the
left hip." Soldiers on horseback were no match for

In December 1914 near
Armentières, weapons
were laid down and a
Christmas truce took
place in 'no man's land'.

machine guns. In the Great War, cavalry
had to take on new roles such
as reconnaissance.

At Ypres the allied front line stuck out into German-held territory. A 'bulge' in trench warfare is called a salient. Soldiers in this part of the trenches can be attacked on three sides.

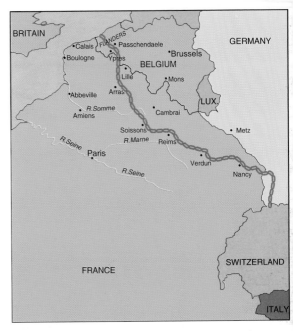

In October 1914 the first battle of Ypres marked the start of trench warfare. Both sides advanced as far as they could and then dug trenches for shelter. Trench warfare led to scenes of slaughter caused by automatic weapons, explosives and poison gas.

Going up out of the trenches into no man's land between the opposing front lines was called going 'over the top'. This meant almost certain death.

23

IN THE TRENCHES

By the end of 1914 the line of opposing trenches stretched from the Belgian coast to the Swiss frontier. This was known as the Western Front. The two 'front lines' were each protected by barbed wire and the area between them was called no man's land. Each trench system had three lines of zigzag trenches. Because the trenches were not straight the impact of explosives was reduced. The front line of each trench system was the firing line, behind this was the support line, and then the reserve line. Communication trenches linked the three lines.

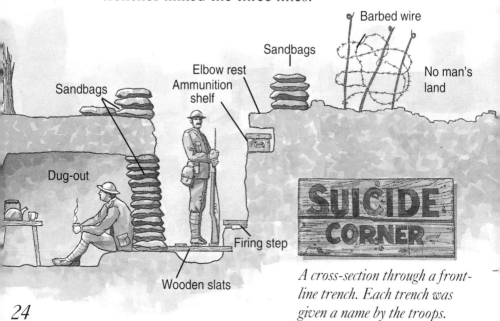

Barbed wire

Sandbags

No man's land

Elbow rest
Ammunition shelf

Sandbags

Dug-out

Firing step

Wooden slats

SUICIDE CORNER

A cross-section through a front-line trench. Each trench was given a name by the troops.

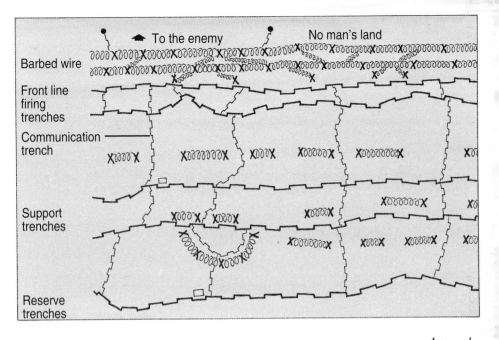

Barbed wire

→ To the enemy

No man's land

Front line
firing
trenches

Communication
trench

Support
trenches

Reserve
trenches

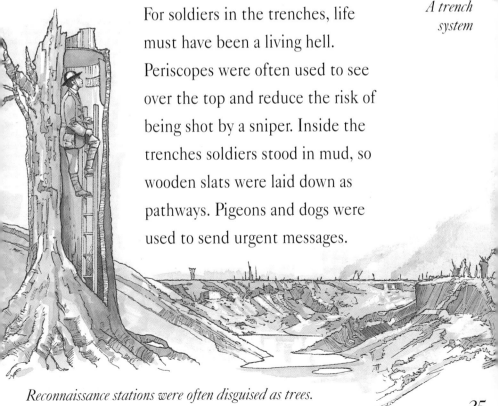

*A trench
system*

For soldiers in the trenches, life must have been a living hell. Periscopes were often used to see over the top and reduce the risk of being shot by a sniper. Inside the trenches soldiers stood in mud, so wooden slats were laid down as pathways. Pigeons and dogs were used to send urgent messages.

Reconnaissance stations were often disguised as trees.

MOVING ABOUT

H orses were desperately needed by the British government during the War. Even horses that were children's pets were commandeered. Troops were carried by train from the coast to the war zones, but there was so much mud on the battlefields that only horses or mules could drag equipment and supplies to the front line. Lorries and trucks became bogged down in the mud. Artillery horses pulled the heavy guns.

THE COTTAGE,
HAIGH,
WIGAN.

Aug: 11th 14.

ear good Lord Kitchener.

We are writing
r our Pony which we are
very afraid may be taken for
your army. Please spare her!
—Daddy says she is going to be
a Mother early next year +
is 17 years old — it would

Three children wrote to Lord Kitchener asking him to spare their pregnant pony, Betty.

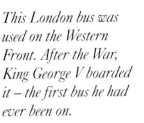

This London bus was used on the Western Front. After the War, King George V boarded it – the first bus he had ever been on.

In the four years of the War, eight million horses died in the most appalling conditions. One of many reasons why the Germans eventually lost the War was because they ran out of horses.

The British 60-pounder field gun could only be moved around by a team of 12 horses.

POISON GAS

The Western Front was the main arena of the Great War. But when Turkey entered the War in 1914, other conflicts arose in important strategic areas like the Dardanelles and Mesopotamia in the Middle East. In 1915 Italy joined the allies. On 22 April 1915, Canadian soldiers in the trenches on the Ypres salient saw a yellow cloud approaching the French lines. The Germans had used poison gas for the first time.

Gas masks and respirators were developed, but some soldiers suffered from the effects of the gas for the rest of their lives.

Built in the 13th century, the Cloth Hall in Ypres was completely destroyed during the Great War. It has since been rebuilt – paid for by Germany.

By 1917 mustard gas was also being used – this caused blindness and burns. The second battle of Ypres continued until May 1915. The Germans advanced, strengthening their defences by building concrete pillboxes on the Messines and Passchendaele ridges.

These pillboxes later proved disastrous for the allies in the third battle of Ypres.

On 25 April 1915 the ill-fated Gallipoli campaign took place in the Dardanelles straits off the coast of Turkey. The Australian and New Zealand Army Corps (ANZAC) suffered heavy losses under Turkish fire. Trench warfare followed until ANZAC were finally evacuated in December 1915.

29

SHIPS AND SUBMARINES

The artist Edward Wadsworth had the idea of painting designs on British ships to confuse enemy submarines.

In 1914 the British navy was the most powerful in the world. When war broke out the British fleet was sent to Scapa Flow in the Orkney Islands. From there, movements to and from German ports could be observed so this was effectively a blockade.

ROYAL NAVAL DIVISION

HANDYMEN TO FIGHT ON LAND & SEA

1ˢᵗ BRIGADE

BATTALIONS:
"BENBOW"
"COLLINGWOOD"
"HAWKE"
"DRAKE"

2ᴺᴰ BRIGADE

BATTALIONS:
"HOWE"
"HOOD"
"ANSON"
"NELSON"

RECRUITS WANTED

RECRUITS WANTED

VACANCIES FOR RECRUITS BETWEEN THE AGES OF 18 AND 38
CHEST MEASUREMENT, 34 · HEIGHT, 5 FT. 3½ IN.
PAYMENT from 1/3 per day. FAMILY ALLOWANCES
Besides serving in the above Battalions and for the Transport
and Engineer Sections attached.
MEN WANTED
who are suitable for Training as Wireless Operators, Signalmen
and other Service with the Fleet.

On 16 December 1914, German warships bombarded the north-east coast of Britain. In Hartlepool 119 people died in a raid lasting 35 minutes. In 1916, German ships entered the North Sea and on 31 May at the battle of Jutland, off the Danish coast, the biggest naval battle of the War was fought. There was no real victor but for the rest of the War the Germans concentrated on U-boat submarine warfare. In April 1917 the German navy sank 354 allied ships. German U-boats blockaded British ports. By September 1917 a convoy system had been introduced because food supplies in Britain were running out.

During the German U-boat blockade, British merchant ships were escorted in convoy by warships.

ANOTHER YEAR OF SLAUGHTER

Carrying the wounded through a sea of mud and water-filled shell holes.

Although there was not much progress on the Western Front during 1915, the number of deaths from trench warfare was still high. 1916 was an even worse year of slaughter. In February the Germans attacked the French at Verdun.

Tanks were first used at the battle of the Somme but not very successfully – 29 of the 50 tanks broke down in the mud.

Verses from a poem written in the trenches.

SING ME TO SLEEP

Sing me to sleep where bullets fall
Let me forget the War and all,
Damp is my dug-out, cold my feet
Nothing but bully and biscuits to eat.

Sing me to sleep where bombs explode
And shrapnel shells are à la Mode,
Over the sandbags helmets you find
Corpses in front and corpses behind.

Far far from Ypres I long to be
Where German snipers can't pot at me,
Think of me crouching where the worms creep
Waiting for someone to sing me to sleep.

Charlie Hay

Despite heavy losses on both sides and a siege lasting many months, Verdun did not fall. On 1 July 1916, British and French troops attacked the Germans along a wide front spanning the River Somme. This offensive went on until 18 November to gain a piece of land measuring only 20 miles long by 6 miles wide. There were 420,000 British, 194,451 French and 650,000 German casualties in a campaign that was doomed to fail.

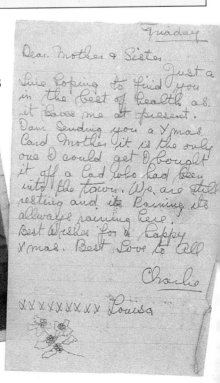

Private Charles Hay, aged 20, was killed at the battle of the Somme.

IN LOVING MEMORY OF
Private CHARLES HENRY HAY,
(3345), 6th D.L.I.;
Dearly Beloved Grandson of Ann Hay, Middridge,
and Son of Thomas Hay,
Who was wounded in Somme Battle in
France, on Sept. 15th.
And died Sept. 18th. 1916.
AGED 20 YEARS.

Friday

Dear Mother & Sister
Just a line hoping to find you in the best of health as it leaves me at present. I am sending you a Xmas Card Mother it is the only one I could get I bought it off a lad who had been into the town. We are still resting and its Raining its always raining here. Best Wishes for a Happy Xmas. Best Love to All

Charlie

XXXXXXXXX Louisa

BALLOONS AND PLANES

The Great War was the first war in which civilians experienced the horror of air raids. War was no longer restricted to the battlefield. Hydrogen-filled airships called Zeppelins were the first airborne threat. In January 1915 two cigar-shaped Zeppelins, 190 metres long, flew over the east coast of England and bombed Great Yarmouth and King's Lynn. Four months later London was targeted. The attacks continued until the introduction of anti-aircraft guns, searchlights and barrage balloons.

Most early aircraft were flimsy and unsafe bi-planes. The pilot was exposed to the air and there were no parachutes. German planes had black crosses on them, while British planes were marked with red, white and blue roundels.

Then in May 1917 the first raids by German Gotha bomber aircraft struck Folkestone on the south coast of England, killing 95 people. There were frequent 'dog fights' over the trenches. In his red Fokker tri-plane, the German pilot Baron von Richthofen shot down 80 allied planes before he was killed in 1918.

At first, bombs were dropped by hand from aircraft. In the early stages of the War, pilots fired at each other in the air with hand guns.

The observation car of a Zeppelin was used when an airship was travelling at high altitudes or above the clouds.

FOOD SHORTAGES

The winter of 1916-17 became known in Germany as the 'turnip winter' because turnips were the only plentiful supply of food. Mobile soup kitchens were a common sight in German streets. In Britain there were no real food shortages for the first two years of the War. But then the German U-boat blockade came into effect and prevented the import of grain. People began to hoard food, prices rose and food queues became common. In April 1917 the British government introduced voluntary food rationing and then compulsory food rationing in 1918.

In Germany, substitute or 'ersatz' materials were used for things like cotton (nettle fibres), coffee (dandelion roots and barley), tea (raspberry leaves), and boot soles (wood instead of leather).

Ration cards meant that everyone received the same amount of food.

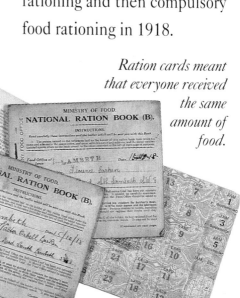

This wartime breakfast recipe was also used as a substitute for potatoes.

Meat was the first food to be rationed, followed by tea, sugar, butter, lard and margarine. Bread and potato prices were fixed and the supply of certain foods like jam and cheese was controlled. Fridays became meatless days and leaflets containing vegetarian recipes were issued.

> ### SAVOURY OATMEAL RISSOLES
> *Take some left-over cold stiff porridge, then mix with dry boiled rice or breadcrumbs made from baked and pounded crusts. Season with pepper and salt and add a few drops of any favourite sauce such as HP or Tomato Ketchup, or flavour with finely chopped herbs and onion. Shape into balls or flat cakes, roll in medium oatmeal and fry in boiling fat. A slice of cooked bacon or ham, minced and mixed in, is a nice addition.*

Tommies accepted that they had to exist on regulation rations at the battle front. But it must have been a shock when they returned home, or to 'blighty' as it was often called, to find that there was food rationing. (A 'ticket for blighty' often meant that a soldier was severely wounded and was being shipped home.)

A WORLD WAR

In June 1917 the Messines Ridge was retaken from the Germans. In late July the British began a major onslaught – the third battle of Ypres. It lasted for three and a half months. The final objective was Passchendaele Ridge. Tommies struggled through mud and German gunfire towards the pillboxes on the ridge. Little was gained in the blood bath that followed. In November the first mass tank attack by the allies took place at Cambrai. The ground gained there was later lost.

A poster from the Russian revolution of 1917.

The third battle of Ypres, also known as Passchendaele, lasted for almost four months.

The Germans sank the Lusitania *on 7 May 1915. 1,201 passengers died, including 128 Americans. Eventually, on 6 April 1917, the USA declared war on Germany. The Great War had truly become a world war. Global conflict was happening for the first time in the history of the world.*

On the Eastern Front the Bolsheviks led a revolution in Russia. In March 1918 Russia and Germany made peace. The Germans were then able to make advances on the Western Front but these were halted by an allied offensive and the arrival of American troops. On 8 August at Amiens, the Germans were driven back.

LEST WE FORGET

The Sinking of the Lusitania.
May 7th 1915.

Over 17,000 North American Indians were part of the American force that reached Europe early in 1918.

PRISONERS AND SPIES

At the beginning of the War the fear of a German invasion of Britain led to the imprisonment of 32,000 enemy aliens as prisoners of war. Local home defence teams were quickly organised all over Britain. Stories of German 'atrocities' in Belgium caused strong anti-German feeling. Everyone was on the look-out for German spies. In 1914, 23 spies were arrested and 11 others were executed before November 1918. In Belgium the English nurse Edith Cavell was in charge of a clinic during the war years. She helped 200 allied fugitives to escape.

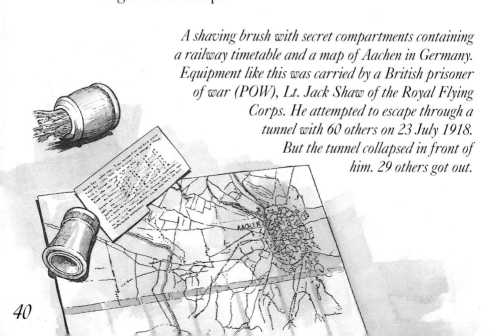

A shaving brush with secret compartments containing a railway timetable and a map of Aachen in Germany. Equipment like this was carried by a British prisoner of war (POW), Lt. Jack Shaw of the Royal Flying Corps. He attempted to escape through a tunnel with 60 others on 23 July 1918. But the tunnel collapsed in front of him. 29 others got out.

Edith Cavell's dog Jack was rescued after she was killed. He died in 1923.

A German court martial found her guilty of spying and she was executed by firing squad in 1915. During the War 160,000 British soldiers were taken prisoner.

An artist's impression of Edith Cavell's death.

Stories of German 'atrocities' in Belgium led to 'spy mania' and anti-German feeling in Britain. Shops and businesses owned by Germans or with German-sounding names were attacked.

PEACE AT LAST

I n September 1918, American troops led the allied offensive to the north west of Verdun. Early in October the British broke through the German front line. By November an armistice had brought fighting to an end. On 9 November the Kaiser abdicated, and at 5 a.m. on 11 November Germany signed the terms of surrender. Six hours later, at 11 a.m., the terms came into effect. The Great War, or the First World War as it had become by then, ended at 11 a.m. on the 11th day of the 11th month, 1918.

A jubilant crowd celebrates the Armistice.

Commemorative mug

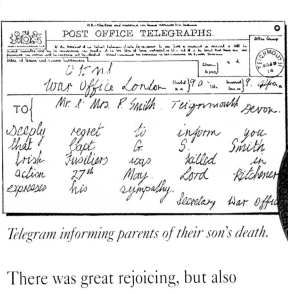

Telegram informing parents of their son's death.

Every family in Britain that had lost a loved one in battle received a next-of-kin medal.

There was great rejoicing, but also immense sadness for the thousands of families who had lost loved ones. In 1919 the Treaty of Versailles was signed and Germany was made to accept blame for the War. An allied army of occupation remained in Germany for a number of years.

Numbers of War Dead 1914-18	
Germany	1,770,000
Russia	1,700,000
France	1,360,000
Austria-Hungary	1,200,000
British Empire	910,000
Italy	460,000
Romania	450,000
Turkey	330,000
Bulgaria	240,000
Serbia	190,000
Belgium	60,000
USA	50,000
Portugal	13,000
Montenegro	13,000

43

THE AFTERMATH

I n November 1918 there were three million British servicemen. By November 1920 there were only 370,000. Many survivors had permanent mental and physical disabilities. Over 240,000 British soldiers had lost limbs. But despite the carnage of the First World War, in 1939 the Second World War began. An attempt had been made to maintain world peace by the American President Woodrow Wilson, who had put forward his 'fourteen points' for a League of Nations organisation. One of his main points had been disarmament, but unfortunately only the Germans had been forced to disarm. This caused great anger among the German people who were already starving and feeling the effects of inflation. It was also one of the reasons why the next world war began.

I KNOW 3 TRADES
I SPEAK 3 LANGUAGES
FOUGHT FOR 3 YEARS
HAVE 3 CHILDREN
AND NO WORK FOR
3 MONTHS
BUT I ONLY WANT
ONE JOB

By 1920 over one million men were unemployed in Britain. This figure remained the same for the next 20 years.

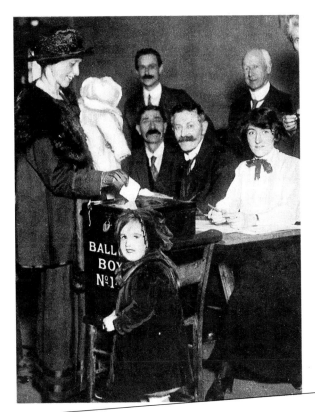

In 1918 all men over the age of 21 and women over the age of 30 in Britain were given the right to vote.

The United Nations(UN) grew out of the League of Nations. UN forces act in a peace-keeping capacity in war-stricken areas all over the world.

UNITED NATIONS TROOPS IN BOSNIA

On the hazardous road to peace

ILLUST

As British soldiers arrive on their mission to bring humanitarian relief to the Balkans, **Michael Evans** examines the tasks and dangers that await them

Arriving at Split from Germany on board an American transport plane, the first 1,000 British soldiers assigned to Operation Grapple, codename for Britain's contribution to the United Nations' humanitarian relief effort in Bosnia, will be met by bewildering contrasts. Wearing flak jackets and helmets, the first batch, due in today, will seem like an invading force to the residents of the pleasant Croatian port.

The soldiers, who have been gearing themselves for a war zone, will not have long to enjoy the peace and relative prosperity of Split. Once they move up through the winding mountainous roads to Vitez in central Bosnia, where the British headquarters is being set up, the picture will change dramatically. Not only that but Vitez been trembling with the sound of gunfire, but the Croats and Muslims, who are to be the British soldiers' neighbours throughout the freezing winter months, have now begun to attack each other.

Politicians and military remain confident that British troops can play a worthwhile part in relieving suffering in Bosnia. The impact on the public at home of the Royal Marines giving food and help to thousands of Kurds trapped in the mountains in northern Iraq last

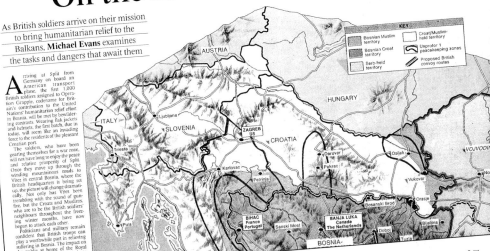

45

Glossary

armistice *A mutual agreement between enemies at war to stop the fighting.*

artillery *Military units trained in the use of heavy guns.*

battalion *A military unit of three or more companies, commanded by a major.*

British Empire *A group of countries once ruled by Britain, now known as the Commonwealth.*

British Expeditionary Force (BEF) *The British army of regular soldiers, numbering 150,000, who left for Belgium in August 1914. 500,000 new volunteers followed within weeks.*

Britannia *Once the symbol of the British Empire – shown as a female warrior carrying a trident and wearing a helmet.*

cavalry *Soldiers on horseback.*

commandeer *To seize for military use.*

conscription *A law passed by the Government of a country stating that men of a certain age have to sign up for military service.*

convoy *A group of merchant ships escorted by warships.*

Eastern Front *The war front to the east of Germany where Russian and German forces confronted each other.*

infantry *Foot soldiers.*

Lord Kitchener *British secretary of war from 1914 to 1916 who created a 'new army' of volunteers.*

Pathé News *The first talking film newsreel, launched in 1908 in France. Now an important source of film archive material.*

reconnaissance *A secret search for information about the enemy during a war.*

Schlieffen Plan *This aimed to achieve a German victory on the Western Front before Russia could mobilise.*

suffragette *A female campaigner of the early 20th century who was determined to gain for women the right to vote.*

tommy *The nickname given to a typical private soldier in the British army.*

Triple Alliance *The alliance signed in 1882 between Austria-Hungary, Germany and Italy.*

Triple Entente *The alliance between France, Britain and Russia, signed in 1908.*

truce *An agreement between enemies to stop fighting temporarily.*

Western Front *The war front to the west of Germany along which trench warfare continued throughout the War.*

INDEX